IT'S NOT A Secret

IT'S NOT A
Secret

James D. Holt

CFI

An imprint of Cedar Fort, Inc.
Springville, Utah

ISBN 13: 978-1-4621-4412-9

Published by CFI, an imprint of Cedar Fort, Inc.
2373 W. 700 S., Suite 100, Springville, UT 84663
Distributed by Cedar Fort, Inc., www.cedarfort.com

Library of Congress Control Number: 2022947376

Cover design by Shawnda T. Craig
Cover design © 2023 Cedar Fort, Inc.

Printed in Colombia

10 9 8 7 6 5 4 3 2 1

Printed on acid-free paper

Introduction

"The temple is a sacred place, and the ordinances in the temple
are of a sacred character. Because of its sacredness we are
sometimes reluctant to say anything about the temple to our
children and grandchildren. As a consequence, many do not
develop a real desire to go to the temple, or when they go there,
they do so without much background to prepare them for the
obligations and covenants they enter into. I believe a proper
understanding or background will immeasurably help prepare
our youth for the temple. This understanding, I believe, will foster
within them a desire to seek their priesthood blessings just as
Abraham sought his." (Ezra Taft Benson, 1985)

As I read these words from President Benson, I am transported back over thirty years to when I joined the Church as a fifteen year old. I was learning so much about the restored gospel of Jesus Christ and I remember going to the missionaries, my Young Men's leaders and my bishop with many questions. Some of them surrounded questions I had about the scriptures: a lot of what I was taught was about how I should live the gospel and become a better disciple of my Saviour Jesus Christ. During the three years of my Church membership before I left on my mission, however, I don't remember being taught much about the temple. We went on quarterly temple visits to perform baptisms and I knew that many of the people I looked up to as role models had been married in the temple—I had a desire to be married in the temple but I'm not sure how much more I knew.

As I went on my mission and entered the London Missionary Training Centre, (MTC) it became very evident how little I knew about the temple of the Lord, what happened therein and why it was important for me to attend the temple and receive my ordinances. At that time, there was only one temple in the UK and I entered the MTC without receiving temple ordinances because the London temple was closed for refurbishment. I wouldn't be able to go to the temple until nearly eighteen months of my mission had passed. I was confused by some of what my fellow missionaries spoke about and the temple garments they wore. It took me a while to work out why people were wearing them and that it wasn't just a coincidence. I think people had not realised that a convert from a household where no one had "gone to the temple" would not understand things that perhaps others took for granted.

Why was there this lack of conversation? Indeed, when I finally went to the temple, I had no real idea what to expect. I did understand the blessings attendant to the temple ordinances and I desired to have claim on those but I think there has always been a reticence to speak about things of the temple for fear of treating lightly those sacred things. I remember a conversation with a ward mission leader when I had been on my mission for nearly a year. He began to say something about an upcoming visit and turned to me and said, "Elder, have you been to the temple?" when I replied in the negative, he swiftly changed the subject.

Over the intervening years, I have served as a bishop and on a Stake Presidency, during that time I have had the opportunity to help people prepare to attend the temple both for the first time as a youth and as adults to receive the further ordinances of the temple. Through these experiences I have come to realise that there is a lot that we can say and do to help children and adults prepare to attend the temple. Sister Reyna Aburto describes coming to a similar realisation:

Sister Reyna Aburto describes coming to a similar realisation:

"Some years ago, my husband Carlos and I were called to teach the temple preparation course in our ward. As part of our calling, our bishop asked us to teach the seventeen-year-old young women and young men about preparing to enter the temple. As we introduced the first lesson to our eager students, we mentioned to them that in the temple we learn about the great plan of salvation. One of the young men, with a look of relief on his face, exclaimed, "Really?! Is that what we learn in the temple? That makes me feel so much better!

"I asked myself, Why has it never occurred to me to teach my children about the temple in a similarly profound and simple way? Why have I denied my children the blessing of hearing more from me the wonderful truths I have learned and the important promises I have made with God in His house through the years?"

This, in a roundabout way, is what has led to the writing of this booklet and has framed the question that will form the basis of our discussion: how can we better prepare our children, our youth and adults to attend the temple? The importance of attending the Lord's house is clear from scriptures and the words of prophets. All of the principles are applicable in different ways to all who would attend the temple. As we discuss the general and specific principles, maybe consider how they apply to your preparation for the temple.

Everything Points to the Saviour

It shouldn't be a surprise as we begin any discussion about preparing to attend the temple that Jesus Christ, the Alpha and the Omega, is the beginning and the end of our discussion. Everything about the temple points us to the Saviour Jesus Christ, and so the best thing that we can do to prepare to attend the temple is to come to know Him and have a testimony of His Atonement and role as Saviour, Mediator and Advocate with the Father. If we have a testimony of His love then we will have a desire to attend His house. The scriptures teach us much about the link between the Lord and His temple:

> *"And inasmuch as my people build a house unto me in the name of the Lord, and do not suffer any unclean thing to come into it, that it be not defiled, my glory shall rest upon it; Yea, and my presence shall be there, for I will come into it, and all the pure in heart that shall come into it shall see God."*
> *(Doctrine and Covenants 97:15–16)*

The temple is the natural next stage in our relationship with our Saviour Jesus Christ. We come to know Him in the daily act of living but this is developed and enhanced in the temple. Defined in context of the plan of salvation, life is a continuum of knowledge where we learn line-upon-line. As we attend the temple and claim its blessings, we can draw closer to Him in a way we had not previously enjoyed.

President Henry B. Eyring has said:

"President Russell M. Nelson made clear for us that we can "see" the Saviour in the temple in the sense that He becomes no longer unknown to us. President Nelson said this: "We understand Him. We comprehend His work and His glory. And we begin to feel the infinite impact of His matchless life." If you or I should go to the temple insufficiently pure, we would not be able to see, by the power of the Holy Ghost, the spiritual teaching about the Saviour that we can receive in the temple." (2021)

For our understanding to be added to, for us to comprehend His matchless life and love, we must have a testimony and understanding of Christ in the first place. We must, in preparing children, youth and adults to attend the temple, place Christ at the centre of all our teaching and example:

"And we talk of Christ, we rejoice in Christ, we preach of Christ, we prophesy of Christ, and we write according to our prophecies, that our children may know to what source they may look for a remission of their sins." (2 Nephi 25:26)

We do this through the way that we teach and the way that we live. When we teach the principles of the gospel, whatever they may be, we must be explicit in our explanation of how they relate to the Saviour. When I explore the teachings of Christianity with my students at University, I begin by asking them to compile a timeline of the events of Jesus' life from the Annunciation to the Ascension. I then have them make a list of all of the actions that Christians perform such as baptism, prayer, partaking of the bread and wine, helping others and so on. Following discussion, I send them away to match up the two lists with the hope that they realise that every action that a Christian performs relates to the life and teaching of the Saviour.

The dedicatory prayer of the Kirtland Temple as recorded in section 109 of the Doctrine and Covenants shows how temple experiences develop our knowledge of the Saviour:

> *"And that they may grow up in thee, and receive a fulness*
> *of the Holy Ghost, and be organized according to thy*
> *laws, and be prepared to obtain every needful thing." (D&C 109:15)*

Whilst we can never fully comprehend the work of the Saviour, in the temple we are able to "grow up" and receive more of a fulness of the Holy Ghost with regard being able to understand Him and His work. As we help others prepare to attend the temple we need to remember that everything points to the Saviour; we need to teach people both the importance of symbolism and the importance of asking purposeful questions.

As members of The Church of Jesus Christ of Latter-day Saints, in our public and private worship we are used to fairly clear symbolism. Consider the use of bread and water as emblems of the sacrament in representing the body and blood of the Saviour. The symbolism of the ordinance of baptism in the burying of the old person/creature, and coming forth as a new creature:

> *"Therefore we are buried with him by baptism into death:*
> *that like as Christ was raised up from the dead by the*
> *glory of the Father, even so we also should walk in*
> *newness of life. For if we have been planted together*
> *in the likeness of his death, we shall be also in the*
> *likeness of his resurrection: Knowing this, that*
> *our old man is crucified with him, that the body*
> *of sin might be destroyed, that henceforth we*
> *should not serve sin." (Romans 6:4-6)*

We explain baptism as representing a new birth, drawing together the elements present at physical birth:

> *"Inasmuch as ye were born into the world by water, and blood, and the spirit, which I have made, and so became of dust a living soul, even so ye must be born again into the kingdom of heaven, of water, and of the Spirit, and be cleansed by blood, even the blood of mine Only Begotten." (Moses 6:59)*

There are many symbols that we perhaps do not give much thought to: the raising of the right hand to sustain; the anointing with oil in the healing of the sick; the laying on of hands and so on. The meaning associated with such symbolism can be found when questions are asked and answers sought from the scriptures and from the Holy Ghost.

Similarly, there are elements of the temple experience where the symbolism is immediately apparent. By dressing in white, for example, we show the equality of all in the eyes of God. This symbolism also helps us understand our relationship with Christ: that through baptism and becoming His, we are unified in His work whatever our background or situation may be.

> *"For as many of you as have been baptized into Christ have put on Christ. There is neither Jew nor Greek, there is neither bond nor free, there is neither male nor female: for ye are all one in Christ Jesus." (Galatians 3:27-28)*

Central to any preparation to enter the Lord's house is to know Him so that we can recognise what we can learn both about Him and from Him. Only by having that burgeoning relationship can we hope to recognise His influence and teachings. Purposeful questioning then, is an essential part of our preparation and our temple experience.

How does what I am seeing, doing, saying point me to Christ?
What am I learning about Christ through these experiences?

This questioning is more important in the temple because not everything is immediately apparent. We have to consider the symbolism of our experience, our actions and words and seek understanding through revelation. We have to be careful about taking this to the extreme, however. After observing the events of creation in a film that was part of the temple experience, I remember one sister talking to me and saying, "Bishop, I'm sorry, I didn't manage to count the number of fish." In seeking symbolism in the minutiae, it is possible for us to miss the "bigger picture."

The Temple in our Homes

We are encouraged, as members of the Church, to have a picture of the temple in our homes and to make the temple an important part of our conversation with our young people. From an early age, our children are taught the importance of the temple through the songs they sing. From the *Children's Songbook* we sing:

> I love to see the temple.
> I'm going there someday
> To feel the Holy Spirit,
> To listen and to pray.
> For the temple is a house of God,
> A place of love and beauty.
> I'll prepare myself while I am young;
> This is my sacred duty.
> (*Children's Songbook*, 95)

In the Latter-day Saint Hymn book we read:

> While I am in my early years,
> I'll prepare most carefully,
> So I can marry in God's temple for eternity.
> (*Hymns*, no. 300)

Making the temple a natural part of our children's lives is essential if we want them to desire to go there. Having a picture of the temple in our homes and perhaps even in our children's rooms helps them connect with the temple. Rather than just a decorative piece, a picture of the temple is a stimulus for discussion as we teach our children about its importance in our lives. My wife and I are fortunate to have been sealed together and so in our home, our sealing certificate is

15

displayed prominently to remind us that we are an eternal family, sealed in God's holy temple. These visual reminders help prompt discussion and serve to remind each member of our family how important the house of the Lord is.

We are also fortunate to live only forty-five minutes from a temple and visit the temple regularly with our children. The Preston temple, where we attend, has beautiful grounds and being in and around the temple as a family, helps us feel at peace and helps us feel the Holy Ghost. We have had picnics in the grounds, walks around the temple—even scavenger hunts to help the children connect with the temple. A trip to a local ice cream shop on the way home sometimes becomes part of our visits too. These small things have helped the temple became a place of happiness, peace and beauty—a place our children all want to go. When we go to the temple, we explain to each of the children about the importance of the temple in our lives; they, in turn, looked forward, anticipating the day of their twelfth birthday when we would be able to go to the temple with them. (Since 2018 youth can now attend the temple at 11).

Prior to their going to the temple for the first time, I would to sit with each of our four children and go through the temple recommend questions with them. For our youngest, I was her bishop but for the other three this was in preparation for their interview with the bishop. None of the principles or topics explored in the recommend questions were new for the children but I wanted them to know what to expect and to have any questions asked of me. This was always a special experience as we discussed the nature of a testimony; the importance of our Saviour; the covenants we make and the commandments we keep. Having this conversation with me was a lovely step on the way to the temple.

Where possible, we took each of our children to the baptistry on their twelfth birthday. When Abi, our second daughter was twelve, her mum was in the hospital that day but we had spoken about it so much as a family, that we decided that even without her mum, it was important for her to be there on that day and enable her to feel of the love and

Spirit in the temple. For our son, his birthday was on a Sunday and having received the priesthood first, we took him on the Tuesday because the temple was closed on the Monday. When it was finally the turn of our youngest, Martha, we all attended the temple together and the love and spirit we felt was indescribable. As I baptised each one of my children for our ancestors there was such a special feeling. I acknowledge that this is not possible for all; when Ruth and I, as converts to the restored gospel, attended the temple first, it was our priesthood leaders who worked with us in the baptistry. Against this background we have always sought to have one or both of us attend the temple with our children. It is imperative that they see that the temple is important to us and we fully support their work and worship in the Lord's house.

As a Bishop helping to prepare each new young woman, new young man or new member of the Church to attend the temple, I was very conscious in the temple recommend interview that each person recognised the blessing it would be. I also endeavoured to ensure that all their needs were catered for as if they were my own child; this included helping them prepare by talking them through many aspects of the experience before them.

As our children grow, we are preparing them for their next steps and often speak of the time when they will receive their endowment and be sealed to their spouse. In order to focus the children on the temple, it is important that Christ is at the centre of all of our discussions. We work on family history and take the opportunity, when it is afforded, to speak of the temple, the blessings we receive by attending the temple and the closeness to the Lord we can feel through the worship and ordinances in which we participate.

In our scripture study we look out for ways to link our reading to the temple. Consider reading the story of Lehi, Sariah and their family as they travel to the promised land. The first activity on arriving at the borders of the Red Sea that they undertake is recorded in 1 Nephi, chapter two:

> *"And it came to pass that he built an altar of stones, and made an offering unto the Lord, and gave thanks unto the Lord our God." (v7)*

And then, later after their second journey back to Jerusalem we read:

> *"And after I and my brethren and all the house of Ishmael had come down unto the tent of my father, they did give thanks unto the Lord their God; and they did offer sacrifice and burnt offerings unto him." (1 Nephi 7:22)*

We also read of similar activities following the split of the sons of Lehi and Sariah into Nephites and Lamanites:

> *"And I, Nephi, did build a temple; and I did construct it after the manner of the temple of Solomon save it were not built of so many precious things; for they were not to be found upon the land, wherefore, it could not be built like unto Solomon's temple. But the manner of the construction was like unto the temple of Solomon; and the workmanship thereof was exceedingly fine." (2 Nephi 5:16)*

Each of these events create easy segues into a discussion about why the temple, altars and sacrifices were of such importance to the Lehites and Nephites. In likening the scriptures to ourselves (1 Nephi 19:23) we are able to begin a discussion about the nature of sacrifice today and the importance of the temple as we go through the journey of life. Some of the scriptural examples may not be as obvious, but we are able, through our own study and understanding to begin to link elements of our teaching to the temple. Consider the many times in the scriptures where people go into the mountain, which became synonymous with a temple experience. We can read of Moses' experience at Sinai; the brother of Jared; Nephi or the Saviour and his disciples at the Mount of Transfiguration. Each of these instances "endowed" the person with new knowledge or a new task—and this can be likened to our own temple experience today.

In addition to the natural conversations that enable us to discuss the temple with our children, President Nelson has suggested topics that might help people as they prepare to attend the temple:

> *"I like to recommend that members going to the temple for the*
> *first time read short explanatory paragraphs in the Bible*
> *Dictionary, listed under seven topics: 'Anoint,' 'Atonement,'*
> *'Christ,' 'Covenant,' 'Fall of Adam,' 'Sacrifices,' and*
> *'Temple.' Doing so will provide a firm foundation."*
> *(Russell M. Nelson, 2001)*

We can begin to teach from a very early age or from a very early stage in the gospel, each of these fundamental principles. Elder Bruce R. McConkie called the Creation, the Fall and the Atonement as the "three pillars of eternity." On these three events hang the plan of salvation that enables all of humanity the opportunity to return and live with our Heavenly Parents.

Teach the Plan of Salvation & Happiness

Returning to the experiences of Sister Aburto and her class of teenagers preparing for the temple, the focus on the plan of salvation is essential. The endowment experience is symbolic of the plan of salvation. With images that are widely available, we are able to talk about the telestial, terrestrial, and celestial rooms—each being expressive of part of our journey. The plan of salvation is central to all of our teaching in preparing people for their temple experience. John A. Widtsoe of the Quorum of the Twelve said:

> *"Temple work . . . gives a wonderful opportunity for keeping alive our spiritual knowledge and strength. . . . The mighty perspective of eternity is unraveled before us in the holy temples; we see time from its infinite beginning to its endless end; and the drama of eternal life is unfolded before us. Then I see more clearly my place amidst the things of the universe, my place among the purposes of God; I am better able to place myself where I belong, and I am better able to value and to weigh, to separate and to organize the common, ordinary duties of my life, so that the little things shall not oppress me or take away my vision of the greater things that God has given us." (1922: 97–98)*

It is important to remember as we teach of the plan of salvation, that Christ stands at the heart of every stage—without Him fulfilling his

21

IT'S NOT A *Secret* by James D. Holt

Father's will and being who He is, the plan of salvation would have come to nought.

Considering the premortal existence, we recognise the primacy of the Saviour as the first born of the Father and the Jehovah of the Old Testament. We learn of his role alongside our Heavenly Parents in teaching all of the human family as they prepared to come to earth. Even in the premortal existence He was our exemplar. We read in Abraham:

> *"And the Lord said: Whom shall I send? And one answered like unto the Son of Man: Here am I, send me. And another answered and said: Here am I, send me. And the Lord said: I will send the first." (3:27)*

This scripture has much to teach us: the second (Satan) was suggesting an alternate plan whereas the first (Jesus) was offering to be the Saviour required by the Father's plan. His perfect obedience began in the premortal existence. Because of the role of the Saviour in the ensuing "war" in heaven, it means that "they who keep their first estate shall be added upon; and they who keep not their first estate shall not have glory in the same kingdom with those who keep their first estate; and they who keep their second estate shall have glory added upon their heads for ever and ever" (Abraham 3:26). In following the Saviour in our first estate of spirit existence, we are able to enter into the second estate of mortality.

This, too, is made possible by the Saviour's obedience to our Heavenly Father and Mother. We learn in the New Testament and Latter-day scripture that the Son was central to Creation. Hebrews tell us:

> *"God, who at sundry times and in divers manners spake in time past unto the fathers by the prophets, Hath in these last days spoken unto us by his Son, whom he hath appointed heir of all things, by whom also he made the worlds." (Hebrews 1:1-2)*

This is expanded in the book of Abraham:

> *"And there stood one among them that was like unto God, and he said unto those who were with him: We will go down, for there is space there, and we will take of these materials, and we will make an earth whereon these may dwell; And we will prove them herewith, to see if they will do all things whatsoever the Lord their God shall command them. (Abraham 3:24-25)*

Mortality and being "prove(d)" does involve a temporary separation from God but the Saviour's Atonement enables us to overcome that separation from the Father. Within the temple, our knowledge of the plan of salvation and the purpose of mortality helps us ask, "What am I learning about my Saviour and how this can draw me close to Him?" The Atonement of the Saviour bridges the gap between the individual and our Heavenly Father. We are drawn into a relationship with Him, His Father and the Holy Spirit as we gain insights during our progression through the endowment in the temple. We can also learn from each action of the Saviour during mortality. As we read this description in Alma, we can recognise this fact:

> *"And he shall go forth, suffering pains and afflictions and temptations of every kind; and this that the word might be fulfilled which saith he will take upon him the pains and the sicknesses of his people." (v11)*

We are all familiar with the pains of our Saviour in the Garden of Gethsemane and on the cross but as we look throughout his life, we also see the pain of friends turning away from Him; the loss of a beloved friend; temptations of all kinds; the harsh words of critics. Indeed, it would seem that one of the only things he didn't experience in his day-to-day life was sin and its consequences which caused him to be "sore amazed" in the garden (Mark 14:33).

Recognising the Saviour's strength for each one of us in mortality enables us to find joy in each day of our journey and prepare for the next stage of existence. The blessings of Jesus' Atonement, however, are not just to be looked forward to; rather they are available to us today. As followers of Christ, the very act of living in mortality enables us to live in a relationship with deity in preparation for the exaltation of eternity.

As we look towards the next stage of mankind's existence and the vicarious work done in temples on behalf of those who have gone before, it is important for us to recognise the temple's pre-eminent role in our lives and "the personal blessing of temple worship" (Howard W. Hunter, quoted in Jay M. Todd, "President Howard W. Hunter," Ensign, July 1994, 5). Through our temple experiences, we are able to receive many personal blessings whilst working to make the temple blessings available to our kindred dead.

The Personal Blessings of Temple Worship

Learning about the personal blessings of temple worship is essential preparation for our children and those people preparing for the temple.

"I hope you would teach this truth about the temple to your children and your grandchildren. Go to the temple—our Father's house—to receive the blessings of your fathers that you may be entitled to the highest blessings of the priesthood.
"For without this no man can see the face of God, even the Father, and live." (D&C 84:22; Ezra Taft Benson, 1985)

The highest motivation for our attendance should be a love of the Saviour and of others but there is also a motivation to be found in recognising the blessings that will come to each of our lives as we attend there and live the covenants that we make therein.

The most important blessing that we can develop within the temple is a closeness to the Father, the Son and the Holy Ghost. We do this through asking ourselves the questions like those listed to earlier and by seeking revelation when we are in the temple. President Hunter has described the temple as "a place of beauty, it is a place of revelation, it is a place of peace. It is the house of the Lord. It is holy unto the Lord. It should be holy unto us" (quoted in Jay M. Todd, 1994: 5). There is no restriction on the revelation that we can receive in the temple as we put ourselves in a place where our minds are less likely to be distracted—and thus we can go to the temple with the questions that concern us. At the end of the temple experience of the endowment, we are able to take time and sit in the celestial room for a time of

25

quiet reflection. I use this opportunity to spend time with my Father in Heaven when I am in this room. Through the conversations I have had with my children, each of them is aware that the temple is a place where I seek revelation and that the broad nature of this revelation is not limited to what is taught there. In The Doctrine and Covenants the Lord teaches:

"For a place of thanksgiving for all saints, and for a

place of instruction for all those who are called to the

work of the ministry in all their several callings and offices;

That they may be perfected in the understanding of

their ministry, in theory, in principle, and in doctrine, in all things

pertaining to the kingdom of God on the earth, the keys of which

kingdom have been conferred upon you." (D&C 97:13-14)

I served as a Bishop for over eleven years and not once during that time did anyone in the temple teach me about my responsibilities as a Bishop; nor did they when I served in other callings, however, I have been instructed by the Lord as to the things that I should do through the revelation I have received. As we go prepared for revelation, we will receive such. We must teach our children the importance of the temple as the one place we can set aside the world and learn the Lord's will for us. We are similarly promised that as we receive this revelation and the peaceful assurance of the Holy Ghost, we will receive strength in our lives:

"Now, my brothers and sisters, we have built temples

throughout the world and will continue to do so. To you

who are worthy and able to attend the temple, I would

admonish you to go often. The temple is a place where

we can find peace. There we receive a renewed dedication

to the gospel and a strengthened resolve to keep the

commandments." (Thomas S. Monson [2009], emphasis added)

Section 109 of The Doctrine and Covenants is one of my favourite scriptures for learning of the blessings of the temple. It is the dedicatory prayer of the Kirtland temple and Howard W. Hunter assured us that this prayer "continues to be answered upon us individually, upon us as families and upon us as a people because of the priesthood power the Lord has given us to use in His holy temples" (Ensign, Oct. 1994: 4). As we consider some of the blessings listed, we realise the significance of temple worship and receiving the ordinances thereof.

The glory of the Lord may rest upon His people

"That thy glory may rest down upon thy people, and upon

this thy house, which we now dedicate to thee, that it

may be sanctified and consecrated to be holy, and that

thy holy presence may be continually in this house;

And that all people who shall enter upon the threshold

of the Lord's house may feel thy power, and feel constrained

to acknowledge that thou hast sanctified it, and that it is

thy house, a place of thy holiness." (D&C 109:12-13)

We can feel the Lord's presence in the temple and that closeness can bring a deeper relationship with each member of the Godhead. In these verses, it outlines that the glory of the Lord will rest down upon His people and His house. What does this mean for each of us as individuals and collectively? There are perhaps two significant ways that the glory of God can be understood. The Bible Dictionary suggests:

"An expression that occurs frequently in the Old Testament.

It sometimes denotes the fulness of the majesty of God,

revealed in the world and made known to men

(Num. 14:21–22; Isa. 6:3; 66:19); in other places it denotes some
outward and visible manifestation of God's presence."
(Ex. 33:17–23; Ezek. 1:28; 9:3; 10:4, 18–19; 11:23;
43:2–5; Luke 2:9; 9:32; John 1:14)

The Presence of the Lord in the Old Testament and in later Jewish thought is often described by the Hebrew word shekhinah. In Jewish thought, this is the idea that God is intimately involved in the daily lives of the people of Israel; He is not some far-removed deity but someone who is mindful of each and every aspect of our lives. Just as the Hebrews were led out of Egypt and in the Exodus by a pillar of fire, so we can be guided and strengthened today.

The second suggestion of what is meant by the Lord's glory is found in Doctrine and Covenants section 93:

"The glory of God is intelligence, or,
in other words, light and truth." (v. 36)

In addition to receiving of His presence, we can also receive "intelligence" or light and truth as we attend and worship in the temple. This is reiterated in the next verses of section 109:

"And do thou grant, Holy Father, that all those who shall
worship in this house may be taught words of wisdom out
of the best books, and that they may seek learning even
by study, and also by faith, as thou hast said; And that
they may grow up in thee, and receive a fulness of the
Holy Ghost, and be organized according to thy laws, and
be prepared to obtain every needful thing." (vv. 14-15)

As explored earlier, our relationship with the Holy Ghost is extended as we experience the temple as a house of learning. We can receive the "mysteries" of God as we focus our worship in the temple. "Mysteries" are those things which can only be known through revelation; the scriptures are replete with references about understanding the mysteries of God, including:

> *"Seek not for riches but for wisdom; and, behold, the mysteries of God shall be unfolded unto you, and then shall you be made rich. Behold, he that hath eternal life is rich." (D&C 11:7)*

I am keen to point out that the "mysteries" are not questions surrounding Adam's tummy button, rather the mysteries are the knowledge of the nature of God, the Atonement of Christ and the basic principles of the gospel of Jesus Christ. Things that should be known through revelation. As we worship in the temple, we are able to "grow up" in our understandings of the gospel principles we have learned throughout our lives. This is an essential aspect to note; we are building line upon line and those who enter the Lord's house must have a basis on which to build.

Furthermore, the knowledge of the mysteries of the kingdom are inextricably linked with the priesthood of the Lord:

> *"The power and authority of the higher, or Melchizedek Priesthood, is to hold the keys of all the spiritual blessings of the church — to have the privilege of receiving the mysteries of the kingdom of heaven, to have the heavens opened unto them, to commune with the general assembly and church of the Firstborn, and to enjoy the communion and presence of God the Father, and Jesus the mediator of the new covenant." (D&C 107:18-19)*

It is no coincidence that the fulness of the priesthood is to be received in the Lord's House through the/an endowment from the Lord. Barbara Morgan Gardner (2019) talks about the two orders of the priesthood, that are complementary, rather than competitive. These two orders are the hierarchical and the patriarchal/familial. We are used to talking about the hierarchical nature of the priesthood and its offices that enables us to establish the nature and order of things within the Church; but less spoken about is the familial nature of the priesthood. This familial order of the priesthood is eternal and has always been; the Doctrine and Covenants teaches us of this truth:

> *"This order [the patriarchal order of the priesthood] was instituted in the days of Adam, and came down by lineage . . . that his posterity should be the chosen of the Lord, and that they should be preserved unto the end of the earth." (Doctrine and Covenants 107:41–42)*

It is important for us to differentiate this endowment of priesthood power and authority from the ordinations received in the hierarchical order of the priesthood. In the temple, people are not ordained to offices but do receive an endowment of the authority and power of the priesthood. Elder M. Russell Ballard (2013) has suggested:

> *"When men and women go to the temple, they are both endowed with the same power, which by definition is priesthood power. While the authority of the priesthood is directed through priesthood keys, and priesthood keys are held only by worthy men, access to the power and the blessings of the priesthood is available to all of God's children."*

Barbara Morgan Gardner outlines this further:

> *"A woman, for example, can go to the temple and receive her endowment and believe she possesses priesthood*

power and authority, and correctly so. Although not ordained
to a priesthood office, she has received this priesthood
power and authority through the ordinances of
the temple." (2019: 18, Deseret Book)

This familial order of the priesthood is a partnership between husband and wife. President Nelson taught:

"Adam held the priesthood, and Eve served in
matriarchal partnership with the patriarchal priesthood."

It is crucial that we understand, however, that this does not mean that only married women are endowed with this power; unmarried women also receive this power through the endowment: its blessings may be fully realised in the future but can be experienced now. I mentioned earlier that I served nearly three quarters of my mission without having received my endowment. Early on in my mission, I studied D&C 109 and became very anxious. How could I serve the Lord effectively without the blessings and endowment promised by the Lord in this prayer? I wrote of my concerns to my Mission President, Joseph Fielding McConkie, who wrote back promising me that no blessing would be held back from me because of circumstances out of my control—though he reminded me that my responsibility was to claim those blessings when the opportunity arose. These promised blessings of priesthood power are available to all on the covenant path, regardless of marital status as they enter the temple.

Although taught throughout the scriptures and in the temple experience itself; it would seem to me that the priesthood blessings and endowment of women is little spoken of and less understood. It is incumbent on us as we teach our children to more fully understand the importance of men and women in the familial priesthood.

Armed with His Power

"And we ask thee, Holy Father, that thy servants may go forth from this house armed with thy power, and that thy name may be upon them, and thy glory be round about them, and thine angels have charge over them. And from this place they may bear exceedingly great and glorious tidings, in truth, unto the ends of the earth, that they may know that this is thy work, and that thou hast put forth thy hand, to fulfil that which thou hast spoken by the mouths of the prophets, concerning the last days." (D&C 109:22-23)

When we speak of the Lord's power, two expressions in the scriptures come to my mind:

1. The power of the Holy Ghost
2. The power of the Priesthood

Interestingly, both are related to the way that we live our lives. We are promised the constant companionship of the Holy Ghost as we keep the commandments and draw close to God; and further in the scriptures we are told that: "the rights of the priesthood are inseparably connected with the powers of heaven, and that the powers of heaven cannot be controlled nor handled only upon the principles of righteousness" (D&C 121:36). If we are to want the power of the Lord in our lives (through the priesthood and through the Holy Ghost) we need to be living righteously or we withdraw ourselves from those blessings (Mosiah 2:36).

The power of the Lord is that which created the world and parted the Red Sea (see D&C 8:2-3). In the daily act of living, we are able to draw on the powers of heaven to develop our relationship with the Saviour and to be strengthened and carried each day of our lives.

33

With this power, section 109 suggests that we have a responsibility to "bear exceedingly great and glorious tidings" to the world. We become missionaries and responsible to warn every nation and people as we enter the Lord's house. More specifically, we are to bear witness to those within our immediate circles of influence. In this task we might wish, along with Alma, we could be more than we are:

> *"O that I were an angel, and could have the wish of mine*
> *heart, that I might go forth and speak with the trump of*
> *God, with a voice to shake the earth, and cry repentance*
> *unto every people! Yea, I would declare unto every soul,*
> *as with the voice of thunder, repentance and the plan*
> *of redemption, that they should repent and come*
> *unto our God, that there might not be more sorrow*
> *upon all the face of the earth." (Alma 29:1–2)*

Yet we do have the same power as the angels:

> *"Do ye not remember that I said unto you that after ye had received*
> *the Holy Ghost ye could speak with the tongue of angels? And now,*
> *how could ye speak with the tongue of angels save it were by the*
> *Holy Ghost? Angels speak by the power of the Holy Ghost;*
> *wherefore, they speak the words of Christ." (2 Nephi 32:2-3)*

With the receiving of the Holy Ghost following baptism and the fulness of the temple we are promised His power to live the covenants we have made.

Angels will have charge over us

Every human, every member of the Church, will find that there are times when we feel alone. The feelings of loneliness may be those that seem to naturally creep up on us as we live our lives or may be the result of belonging to a "minority branch" of Christianity. Finding ourselves the only Church member in our school, work, family or friendship group can present us with challenges but we are promised that angels will have charge over us. This is illustrated in the experiences of the first missionaries to the British Isles:

"About daybreak, Brother Russel[l] . . . called upon us [Heber
C. Kimball and Orson Hyde] to rise and pray for him,
for he was . . . afflicted with evil spirits. . . . We immediately
arose and laid hands upon him and prayed that the Lord
would have mercy on his servant and rebuke the devil;
while thus engaged, I was struck with great force by
some invisible power and fell senseless on the floor. . . .
[A vision was opened to our minds and we] could distinctly
see the evil spirits who foamed and gnashed their teeth
upon us. . . . I perspired exceedingly, and my clothes were
as wet as if I had been taken out of the river. . . .
By [this experience] I learned the power of the
adversary [and] his enmity against the servants of God
and got some understanding of the invisible world. However,
the Lord delivered us from the wrath of our spiritual enemies
and blessed us exceedingly that day, and I had the pleasure . . .
of baptizing nine individuals." (R. B. Thompson ed. [1840]: 19;
spelling and punctuation standardised)

35

Although he had a vision of the "infernal" worlds, we know that the angels that have charge over us are more numerous than those that assail us. We have angels who strengthen us and guide us so that the promises of the scriptures can be claimed:

"No weapon formed against them shall prosper; that he who diggeth a pit for them shall fall into the same himself; That no combination of wickedness shall have power to rise up and prevail over thy people upon whom thy name shall be put in this house." (D&C 109:25-26)

Returning to those angels of which the scriptures promise will be with us; Elder Jeffrey R. Holland (2008) clarifies who these may be:

"I have spoken here of heavenly help, of angels dispatched to bless us in time of need. But when we speak of those who are instruments in the hand of God, we are reminded that not all angels are from the other side of the veil. Some of them we walk with and talk with—here, now, every day. Some of them reside in our own neighbourhoods. Some of them gave birth to us, and in my case, one of them consented to marry me. Indeed heaven never seems closer than when we see the love of God manifested in the kindness and devotion of people so good and so pure that angelic is the only word that comes to mind."

Each of us, through the endowment of the priesthood have claim on the ministering of angels and receive of those blessings daily as we keep the covenants that we have made. There are many temptations that Satan and his minions will throw at us but we know that as children of God, we have the strength within and around us to withstand these temptations. This strength can come, not least, because in the temple we come to know fully who—and whose, we are. This is best exemplified in the experiences of Moses with the Lord and with Satan. In Moses 1 we read of the Lord's interaction with Moses that highlights Moses' identity:

> *"And, behold, thou art my son." (Moses 1:4)*

> *"And I have a work for thee, Moses, my son; and thou art*
> *in the similitude of mine Only Begotten; and mine Only*
> *Begotten is and shall be the Saviour. (Moses 1:6)*

> *"And now, behold, this one thing I show unto thee,*
> *Moses, my son. (Moses 1:7)*

We learn of our identity through the scriptures, through the hymns we sing and in the temple of the Lord. We know we are each individual children of God. We are also able to know of our nothingness in comparison to Him but also know that we are everything to Him. This is exemplified in the effects of the time spent with the Lord on Moses:

> *"And the presence of God withdrew from Moses, that his*
> *glory was not upon Moses; and Moses was left unto*
> *himself. And as he was left unto himself, he fell unto the*
> *earth. And it came to pass that it was for the space of*
> *many hours before Moses did again receive his natural*
> *strength like unto man; and he said unto himself: Now,*
> *for this cause I know that man is nothing, which*
> *thing I never had supposed." (Moses 1:9-10)*

We then read of Satan's attempts to tempt Moses, and how knowing his divine identity means that Moses is able to withstand anything that is thrown at him:

> *"Satan came tempting him, saying: Moses, son of*
> *man, worship me." (Moses 1:12)*

Satan tries to reduce Moses to a mere man; but armed with a knowledge of who he is Moses responds:

> *"And it came to pass that Moses looked upon Satan and*
> *said: Who art thou? For behold, I am a son of God, in*
> *the similitude of his Only Begotten; and where is thy*
> *glory, that I should worship thee?... Get thee hence, Satan;*
> *deceive me not; for God said unto me: Thou art after*
> *the similitude of mine Only Begotten." (Moses 1:13, 16)*

This theme is repeated throughout the scriptures and throughout our lives. When he asked who the crowd thought he should release, Pilate presented Jesus (the Son of God) and Barabbas (the son of a man). The crowd chose the mundane over the sacred. We are faced with this same choice as we are faced with the temptations of life; do we trust in the arm of flesh or in the arm of the Lord? It is only by building on a sure foundation rather than the sand that we can allow God to prevail in our lives and thus prevail ourselves. This truth is taught clearly in The Book of Mormon:

> *"And now, my sons, remember, remember that it is upon*
> *the rock of our Redeemer, who is Christ, the Son of God,*
> *that ye must build your foundation; that when the devil*
> *shall send forth his mighty winds, yea, his shafts in*
> *the whirlwind, yea, when all his hail and his mighty*
> *storm shall beat upon you, it shall have no power*
> *over you to drag you down to the gulf of misery and*
> *endless wo, because of the rock upon which ye are built,*

which is a sure foundation, a foundation whereon if

men build they cannot fall." (Helaman 5:12)

When we teach our children the blessings that we find through worshipping in the temple, they cannot help but recognise the spirit and power that comes into our lives. We should take every opportunity to testify of the Saviour and the blessings of attending His house.

The Spirit World

After we have received our own temple blessings, we worship in the temple on behalf of those who passed on from this world without receiving the ordinances of the gospel of Jesus Christ. Although we often talk about going to the temple for the first time as referring to receiving our endowment; for the vast majority of people their first time at the temple is the baptistry. Regular attendance at the temple baptistry as a young person or new member provides as much as a link to the spirit world as when we perform other ordinances in the temple. The first initiatory and endowment ordinances we receive are for ourselves but every other time we worship in the temple (except for temple sealing of living spouses and children) are on behalf of our ancestors who are in the Spirit World and have not have the opportunity to receive some/all of the ordinances of exaltation while in this life.

President Thomas S. Monson (2009) highlighted the importance and blessings of such service:

"What a privilege it is to be able to go to the temple, where

we may experience the sanctifying influence of the

Spirit of the Lord. Great service is given when we

perform vicarious ordinances for those who have gone

beyond the veil. In many cases we do not know those

for whom we perform the work. We expect no thanks, nor

do we have the assurance that they will accept that

which we offer. However, we serve, and in that process

we attain that which comes of no other effort: we literally

become saviours on Mount Zion. As our Saviour gave His

life as a vicarious sacrifice for us, so we, in some small

measure, do the same when we perform proxy work in

the temple for those who have no means of moving

forward unless something is done for them by those of

us here on the earth."

In the temple the connection with the spirit world is sometimes palpable as we complete vicarious work. We should be as excited to perform this work as were the first Saints. It has been said that Joseph Smith first preached on the topic of baptism for the dead at the funeral of Seymour Brunson in 1840 and there is the suggestion that people ran to perform the baptisms for their loved ones immediately following this sermon. Whatever the precise circumstances, journals record hundreds of baptisms being performed and that necessitated an order being established and the work moving to the temple on its completion.

Finding ancestors to take to the temple through researching our family history is an "easy" way to get people involved in the work of the temple. As people "find" members of their family they become eager to participate in the temple work for them. This is not something that we can leave to those in our family who have a special interest but is something that we all need to do. The promises made by Moroni to Joseph Smith affect us all:

"Behold, I will reveal unto you the Priesthood, by the hand

of Elijah the prophet, before the coming of the great

and dreadful day of the Lord. And he shall plant in the

hearts of the children the promises made to the fathers,

and the hearts of the children shall turn to their fathers.

If it were not so, the whole earth would be utterly

wasted at his coming." (D&C 2:1-3)

In the binding of the generations of our family, we come to realise, along with Joseph Smith that "For we without them cannot be made perfect; neither can they without us be made perfect." (D&C 128:18)

I am always touched when I read Doctrine and Covenants 138 and the events that surrounded its revelation. Knowing that President Joseph F. Smith was mourning the loss of his son makes the revelation all the more poignant and needed. He saw the work that continues in the spirit world after death. Moroni said to the Prophet Joseph:

"Foreshadowing the great work to be done in the temples

of the Lord in the dispensation of the fulness of times,

for the redemption of the dead, and the sealing of the

children to their parents, lest the whole earth be

smitten with a curse and utterly wasted at his coming."

(D&C 138:48)

In our home there have been many discussions about these principles; the importance of Family History and the work in the temple that will bind us together. My father died when I was three, many years before I was baptised or even heard about the Church. When we joined the Church, this was one of the great comforts to me as I understood the eternal nature of our relationship. Although I have only one or two memories of him, I know that if he accepts the gospel, we can spend eternity developing the relationship that we missed out on here. Knowing that I am now sealed to him and my mum makes life sweeter. God loves all of his children and desires exaltation and eternal family relationships for each of them. This binding/sealing together of families through the ordinances available in the temple is a great blessing and responsibility and it should be talked of often in our homes.

The blessings that come because of this sealing of families have been never clearer to me than when I have spoken at funerals over the years. Two stand out in particular: the funerals of Martin and Finley who both died within moments of their birth. Speaking at each of their funerals I was faced with the enormity of how I could offer comfort to their families. Fortunately, comfort doesn't come through me but through the Atonement of the Saviour mediated through the Holy Ghost. President Joseph F. Smith taught:

"The mother who laid down her little child [in a grave],
being deprived of the privilege, the joy, and the satisfaction
of bringing it up to manhood or womanhood in this world,
would after the resurrection, have all the joy, satisfaction
and pleasure, and even more than it would have been
possible to have had in mortality, in seeing her child
grow to the full measure of the stature of its spirit...
It matters not whether these tabernacles mature in
this world, or have to wait to mature in the world to come...
the body will develop either in time or in eternity, to the
full stature of the spirit, and when the mother is
deprived of the pleasure and joy of rearing her babe
to manhood or womanhood in this life, through the
hand of death, that privilege will be renewed to her
hereafter, and she will enjoy it to a fuller fruition than it
would be possible for her to do here. When she does it
there, it will be with certain knowledge that the results

will be without failure; whereas here, the results are
unknown until after we have passed the test." (1939: 452-54)

What greater comfort can we have than this? It reminds me of an occasion where I was invited to speak to a local Methodist women's group and introduce our Church to them. I taught of the Saviour and the plan of salvation. A lady approached me afterward concerned about her resurrection. She was an older lady and her husband had died forty years previously. She worried that when she was resurrected, her husband wouldn't want such an old lady. This is a blessing that our knowledge of the resurrection brings: we know that our perfected, resurrected body not only helps put us beyond Satan's power forever but it enables us to have the "same sociality" that we have had here.

Learning about the links between the Spirit World and the temple will both prepare us for the temple and motivate us to attend there. I have felt a special spirit when we are completing work as a family, for members of our family. In such instances, I find it important, when I am in the font, to explain to the person I am baptising who they are being baptised for and the link to their family or another family in the ward.

The Degrees of Glory

I was once teaching with the missionaries and they shared the plan of salvation up until the Spirit World and appeared to end there. Maybe it makes sense as it links with other Christian understandings of life after death with the separation to paradise and prison but at that point I couldn't hold back. I explained that there was much more to know. The judgement of the Lord is not binary; following a resurrection and judgement we are assigned a kingdom of glory because we kept our first estate (the premortal existence). Moreover, I explained that in the celestial kingdom we are united as families with the Father and the Son. What greater blessing is there than this?

Our experiences in the telestial, terrestrial, and celestial rooms are central to our temple worship. Understanding that there are degrees of glory enables a person to begin to understand the journey of their temple endowment experience. The symbolism and the teachings of the endowment encourage people to reflect on where they came from and hopefully, where they are going. Without an understanding of the plan of salvation, a person will not be prepared for the ordinances that they will receive in the temple both for themselves and on behalf of others. The various phases of the endowment help a person draw closer to Christ and understand their ultimate destiny.

Teach the ordinances of salvation

The ordinances of salvation are not secret; as has been said many times, they are sacred. To keep them shrouded in mystery will not help prepare our children and others for the temple.
Elder Robert D. Hales taught:

"The primary purpose of the temple is to provide the ordinances necessary for our exaltation in the celestial kingdom. Temple ordinances guide us to our Saviour and give us the blessings that come to us through the Atonement of Jesus Christ." (2009: 48)

If the purpose of the temple is to receive the ordinances that will guide us to the Saviour; those who attend the temple should strive to understand them. The ordinances outside of baptism and confirmation are described by Gordon B. Hinckley (1982):

"These temple blessings include our washings and anointings that we may be clean before the Lord. They include the instruction service in which we are given an endowment of obligations and blessings that motivate us to behavior compatible with the principles of the gospel. They include the sealing ordinances by which that which is bound on earth is bound in heaven, providing for the continuity of the family."

Initiatory Ordinances

Preparing to Enter the Holy Temple explains:

"Associated with the endowment are washings and anointings— mostly symbolic in nature, but promising definite, immediate blessings as well as future blessings. In connection with these ordinances, in the temple you will be officially clothed in the garment and promised marvellous blessings in connection with it. It is important that you listen carefully as these ordinances are

administered and that you try to remember the blessings promised and the conditions upon which they will be realised."

We can explain, as appropriate, that the symbolic act of washing and anointing promises blessings to each of us based on covenants that we make. A focus on the fact that we are making covenants and that we will receive blessings through those ordinances will enable children to recognise that in some ways it is no different from the ordinances of baptism, confirmation and ordination to the priesthood.

In helping prepare others to receive the blessings of the temple, we also should talk of temple garments; the Church has produced videos to outline their importance and use. Our children will probably be familiar with them if they live in a home with endowed parents and/or siblings and can learn that these are a sacred symbol and reminder of our covenants. The temple recommend reminds us that they "are an outward expression of an inward commitment to follow the Saviour."

The experience shared in *Preparing to Enter the Holy Temple* of a General Authority speaking to a group of clergy helps contextualise a further reason for wearing the garment:

He said, "In civilian life and also when conducting the meetings in the military service you wear clerical clothing, do you not?"
The chaplain said that he did.

He continued: "I would suppose that that has some importance to you, that in a sense it sets you apart from the rest of your congregation. It is your uniform, as it were, of the ministry. Also, I suppose it may have a much more important place. It reminds you of who you are and what your obligations and covenants are.

It is a continual reminder that you are a member of the clergy,

that you regard yourself as a servant of the Lord, and that you are

responsible to live in such a way as to be worthy of your ordination."

It is just so with our wearing of the garment; they are physical reminders of who we are, our covenants and our relationship with the Lord.

The Endowment

The focus on the Saviour and the plan of salvation, while evident in the initiatory and sealing ordinances, are brought into particular focus in the endowment. As we look at the images of the various rooms of the temple, we can see that the endowment involves receiving instruction regarding:

- The Creation of the world
- The Fall of Adam and Eve
- The Atonement of Jesus Christ
- The Apostasy
- The Restoration
- The way all people can return to the presence of the Lord

In the endowment there are opportunities to learn through the symbolism of how we worship, what we see and the clothing that we wear. As part of the temple endowment experience, we also make covenants with the Lord, which include:

- Law of Obedience
- Law of Sacrifice
- Law of the Gospel
- Law of Chastity
- Law of Consecration

Elder James E. Talmage has suggested:

"The ordinances of the endowment embody certain obligations on the part of the individual, such as covenant and promise to observe the law of strict virtue and chastity, to be charitable, benevolent, tolerant and pure; to devote both talent and material means to the spread of truth and the uplifting of the race; to maintain devotion to the cause of truth; and to seek in every way to contribute to the great preparation that the earth may be made ready to receive her King—the Lord Jesus Christ. With the taking of each covenant and the assuming of each obligation a promised blessing is pronounced, contingent upon the faithful observance of the conditions." (1976: 84)

None of these are new covenants to us; but making them in the temple adds a greater responsibility on each of us to live these covenants. We don't suddenly find new aspects to the law of chastity and tithing does not suddenly "go up" . . . rather, the covenants are made with a renewed spirit that suggests the importance of the Lord's revelation that: "For of him unto whom much is given much is required." (D&C 82:3)

The Church's website tells us of the temple endowment:

"At the conclusion of the endowment, participants symbolically return to the Lord's presence as they enter the celestial room. There you can spend time to ponder, pray, read the scriptures, or quietly discuss your experiences with family and friends. It is a place of peace, where you can also find comfort and divine direction."

It is important that as we spend time in the celestial room of the temple, we take the opportunity to commune with the Lord. Time to "Be still, and know that I am God" (Psalm 46:10). I have often seen people walk into the room and walk straight back out again but if we can make the most of the time we have in the temple, we can find the peace we are promised.

Sealing

The sealing is often described as the crowning ordinance of the gospel. The Lord has revealed:

> *"If a man marry a wife by my word, which is my law, and by the new and everlasting covenant, and it is sealed unto them by the Holy Spirit of promise, by him who is anointed, unto whom I have appointed this power and the keys of this priesthood; . . . and if [they] abide in my covenant, . . . it shall be done unto them in all things whatsoever my servant hath put upon them, in time, and through all eternity; and shall be of full force when they are out of the world."*
>
> *(D&C 132:19)*

Of note here, is that in this ordinance, a couple is sealed by the Holy Spirit of promise. This means that the seal is affixed but is not made certain except by faithfulness to the covenants that are made between the Lord and the couple. Sometimes, people may regard the sealing ordinance, because it is the "crowning" blessing, as an end—but it is only a step and not even the final step on the path to exaltation. It is no surprise that the Lord's servants have been speaking more of the importance of the covenant path in recent years.

This lesson was taught to me as I prepared to get married and sealed to Ruth. My bishop approached me and invited me to me to go on the Institute: Achieving a celestial marriage course. I flippantly replied,

"It's okay, Bishop. I have that one covered. I get sealed in a couple of months." Flippancy wasn't really this Bishop's thing, but I have always remembered his reply, "James, in a couple of months you will have a temple marriage but whether it is a celestial marriage will be determined throughout your life and the eternities." He offered that wise counsel and it has stuck with me over the years. We haven't arrived, we just have the tickets.

As with all ordinances, the sealing ordinance of husband and wife and the sealing of children to their newly sealed parents, draws us to the Saviour and teaches us about his Atonement.

Elder Bruce C. Hafen (2015) noted when sealing a couple in the temple:

"I invited them to the altar, and as the groom took the bride by the hand, I realised that they were about to place upon that altar of sacrifice their own broken hearts and contrite spirits—an offering of themselves to each other and to God in emulation of Christ's sacrifice for them. By living that way every day, they would each come closer to God, which would also bring them closer to each other. Thus, living the covenants of the sealing ordinance would sanctify not only their marriage but also their hearts and their very lives."

These things should influence the way that we live our lives and the way that we attend the temple as we consider not only our own relationship with the Saviour, but also that of our family.

Final Thoughts

The "simple" thing we can do to help prepare others to enter the holy temple is to talk about the temple; the temple should not be a taboo subject in our homes. Of course this is easier if we have received those ordinances ourselves but as we take the opportunity to, first and foremost, link all of our teaching to the Saviour Jesus Christ, we will prepare our children to do exactly the same thing as they enter the temple. They will be prepared to ask the question that they will have been asking their whole life: "What am I learning about the Saviour and how does this draw me closer to Him?"

Preparing for the temple does require a relationship with the Saviour to help us reach our goal. I have seen many people seem to get close to the point of attending the temple but stumble before roadblocks in their way. I have learnt that opposition is real and that everyone has their agency. Drawing our temple experiences and preparation for the temple to the centrality of the Saviour and his Atonement is what will get us through.

To encourage others, we can talk of our attendance at the temple, of the blessings we receive through our worship there and about how so many of the gospel principles we learn, link to the temple. We don't need to shoehorn everything that we ever teach to into a discussion about the temple but we should teach about the temple often. President Nelson indicated (above) that there are many things in the scriptures that link easily to the experience of temple worship.

53

Just as a love of the Saviour and of the temple is crucial in helping people feel a desire to go to the temple; so too the binding of generations is key. We can involve children in family history at any age. Knowing why they are doing temple work will increase their, and our, desire. We should speak often of the blessings we receive through the ordinances of the temple and the associated covenants, including the ordinances of baptism and confirmation that are the first temple ordinances many people will experience.

Ultimately, the idea is to develop "I love to see the temple" into "I love to attend the temple." If we teach children and new temple attendees about the temple in a way that prepares them to feel the Holy Spirit and draw close to the Saviour as they attend, they will find that the blessings of the temple are open to all—and they certainly are.

About the Author

Who is JAMES D. HOLT?

James Holt is Associate Professor of Religious Education at the University of Chester. He is married to Ruth and they are the parents of four children (now five after a recent wedding). He holds a PhD in Latter-day Saint theology from the University of Chester. He served a mission in the Scotland Edinburgh Mission and has served as a bishop, in a stake presidency, and on the curriculum writing committee of the Church for *Teachings of the Presidents of the Church: Gordon B. Hinckley*. He is the author of *Hearing Him* and *Gospel Lessons from my Heroes*.

Resources:

Aburto, Reyna (2020). *Reaching for the Savior*, Deseret Book.

Ballard, M. Russell (2013). "Let Us Think Straight," BYU Speeches, Aug. 20, 2013.

Benson, Ezra Taft (1985). "What I Hope You Will Teach Your Children about the Temple." Address given at the Logan Temple Centennial, May 17, 1984; *Ensign*, Aug. 1985.

Eyring, Henry B. (2021). "I Love to See the Temple," April 2021 general conference.

Hafen, Bruce R. (2015). "The Temple and the Natural Order of Marriage," *Ensign*, Sept. 2015.

Hales Robert D. (2009). "Blessings of the Temple," *Ensign*, Oct. 2009.

Holland, Jeffrey R. (2008). "The Ministry of Angels," *Ensign*, Nov. 2008.

Hinckley, Gordon B. (1982). "Temples and Temple Work," *Ensign*, Feb. 1982.

Hunter, Howard W. (1994). "The Great Symbol of our Membership," *Ensign*, Oct. 1994.

Monson, Thomas S. (2009). "Until We Meet Again," *Ensign*, May 2009.

Morgan Gardner, Barbara (2019). *The Priesthood Power of Women: In the Temple, Church, and Family*, Deseret Book.

Nelson, Russell M. (1987). "Lessons from Eve," *Ensign*, Nov. 1987.

Nelson, Russell M. (2001). "Personal Preparation for Temple Blessings," *Ensign*, May 2001.

Smith, Joseph F. (1939). *Gospel Doctrine*, Deseret Book.

Todd, Jay M. (1994). "President Howard W. Hunter," *Ensign*, July 1994.

Widstow, John A. (1922). In Conference Report, April 1922.

Talmage, James E. (1976). *The House of the Lord*, rev. ed.

Thompson, R. B., ed. (1840). Journal of Heber C. Kimball.

Notes

Notes